Messages from the Stars: A Guide to Summoning the Galactic Federation

Jessie Contreras

Published by Summon UFOs, 2024.

MESSAGES FROM THE STARS: A GUIDE TO SUMMONING THE GALACTIC FEDERATION

First edition. September 11, 2024.

Copyright © 2024 Jessie Contreras.

ISBN: 979-8227489746

Written by Jessie Contreras.

Table of Contents

"This book is dedicated to all the daring and inquisitive souls who seek to connect with the unknown and reach out to the beings beyond our realm. May your journey into the depths of the cosmos be filled with wonder, curiosity, and the courage to question the mysteries of the universe. Together, let us summon the Galactic Federation and embark on a journey of discovery beyond our wildest dreams."

Chapter 1: The Call of the Stars

1.1 The Mystique of UFOs

The history of UFO phenomena is richer and more complex than most people realize. Accounts of unexplained flying objects stretch back centuries, deeply intertwined with human culture and mythology. From the fiery chariots noted in ancient texts to the famous Roswell incident in 1947, these mysterious sightings often ignite the imagination. They pose intriguing questions about our place in the universe and what—or who—might be watching us. Cultural significance cannot be overstated; societies around the globe have created narratives that shape beliefs, often blending science with spirituality. The stories of abductions, encounters, and government cover-ups have drawn many of us into a world where reality mingles with fantasy, where curiosity fuels a search for truth about the cosmos.

I often find myself reflecting on how these mysteries sparked my own fascination with space and the possibility of extraterrestrial life. There's something utterly captivating about looking up at the night sky, contemplating the vastness above, and wondering if we are truly alone. Each strange light or fleeting shadow can evoke a deep sense of wonder and possibility. The more I learned, the more I felt a pull to explore the unknown. My evenings turned into sessions of stargazing, where every twinkle held the promise of something unexplainable. I started to seek out gatherings where like-minded individuals shared their experiences and theories—people who also felt a connection to the Galactic Confederation of Light. The idea that we might not only be visitors to the cosmos but also active participants in a grand cosmic community inspired me to delve deeper.

This journey has taught me that the beauty of these phenomena lies not just in their mystery but also in their ability to bring people together.

Each encounter, each story shared, fuels a collective inquiry into our existence. For anyone intrigued by these celestial guests, I recommend spending quiet nights under the stars with an open heart and mind. Create a space for intuition and connection; consider meditative practices that resonate with you. Drawing on the energy of the cosmos can help illuminate your path while inviting a deeper understanding of the mysteries that lie beyond our world.

1.2 Unveiling the Galactic Federation

The notion of a Galactic Federation has been a topic of intrigue and wonder for many who feel a connection to the stars and the broader universe. This federation, often described as a coalition of advanced extraterrestrial civilizations, operates under the principles of peace, cooperation, and mutual growth. Imagine a vast tapestry of intelligent beings from different worlds, coming together to ensure a cohesive and harmonious existence. They are dedicated to uplifting less advanced civilizations while also respecting their autonomy and unique paths. The implications of such a federation are monumental; they suggest that our understanding of life, consciousness, and collaboration can expand far beyond our current limits. It challenges us to consider the vastness of existence and our role within it, revealing endless possibilities for connection and understanding beyond Earth.

Diving deeper into the essence of the Galactic Federation, many spiritual texts and channeling experiences shed light on the nature of this cosmic alliance. These messages often emphasize a mission that transcends mere coexistence. They reveal a commitment to enlightenment, healing, and the elevation of consciousness across the universe. Channeling sessions, where individuals connect with higher beings or wisdom, frequently relay themes of love, compassion, and unity. The Galactic Federation is portrayed as a nurturing force, guiding humanity towards a greater awakening. Participants in these channelings report feelings of profound peace and connection, as if they were receiving wisdom from ancient sources. This celestial council encourages us to tap into our intrinsic potential and align with a higher frequency of love and understanding.

For those interested in actively connecting with the Galactic Federation or inviting their presence, a practical approach is to cultivate an open heart and mind. Meditations focused on receiving universal love can create a resonance that may attract benevolent forces. Visualization techniques can be powerful tools; envisioning a bright, welcoming light surrounding you can help signal your intention to connect. It's essential to remain grounded and centered while being open to the incredible possibilities that lie beyond our physical reality. Trusting in the process and maintaining a vibration of positivity can enhance the experience of summoning these benevolent extraterrestrial entities into our lives.

1.3 My First Encounter with the Unknown

The night sky was unusually clear, dotted with countless stars that twinkled like diamonds scattered across a velvet canvas. I remember standing outside, feeling a sense of calm mixed with anticipation. Suddenly, a flash of silver caught my eye—a small, gleaming object darted across the horizon, moving with a speed that defied earthly understanding. My heart raced, pounding in my chest as I struggled to process what I was witnessing. Was it a shooting star? A plane? No, this was something else entirely. It shifted direction abruptly, leaving me breathless and awestruck, emotions swirling like a tempest within me. Excitement ignited my spirit, followed closely by a flicker of fear. What was this phenomenon? As it vanished just as quickly as it had appeared, it left an indelible mark on my psyche—a thirst for understanding, an urge to communicate with the unknown.

This encounter transformed my journey, steering me toward a path laden with fascination and inquiry about interstellar beings. I found myself consumed by questions: Who or what inhabited that fleeting object?

What messages were they sending? Each night thereafter, I took to the skies, hoping to reconnect with that shimmering enigma. I began exploring literature on UFOs, diving deep into the accounts of others who had experienced similar phenomena. Forums filled with passionate believers, techniques for summoning, and discussions surrounding the Galactic Confederation of Light became my sanctuaries. Those initial feelings of fear transformed into a profound sense of purpose as I realized that I wasn't alone in my quest for cosmic awareness. My life became a tapestry woven with the threads of strange encounters, insights, and a growing network of like-minded souls.

To enhance the possibility of such encounters, I learned the importance of setting intentions. Each time I gazed into the stars, I mentally invited these beings to connect. I envisioned a warm light surrounding me, creating a benevolent space for communication. This practice not only helped me cultivate patience and hope but also deepened my understanding of the universe and my place within it. Remember, the cosmos listens. Your thoughts, feelings, and desires can resonate across the vastness of space, drawing closer the unknown that you seek.

Chapter 2: Understanding the Galactic Confederation

2.1 Who Are the Beings of Light?

Beings of light are incredibly fascinating entities that transcend our conventional understanding of existence. They often appear as radiant, luminescent figures, embodying a spectrum of colors that seem to shift and shimmer with their emotions or intentions. Their presence is described as warm and reassuring, radiating a profound sense of peace and unconditional love that envelops those who encounter them. Many people report feelings of euphoria, clarity, and connection to something much greater than themselves when in their presence. These beings carry attributes such as compassion, wisdom, and heightened awareness. Unlike humans, who may be bogged down by limitations and fears, beings of light operate from a place of pure intention and love, often serving as mentors or guardians for those on a spiritual path.

The Galactic Confederation encompasses a diverse array of species, each with unique capabilities and contributions to the whole. Among them are the Arcturians, known for their advanced healing techniques and deep metaphysical knowledge. These beings often step forward as teachers, guiding us in our spiritual development and helping us to awaken dormant aspects of our consciousness. The Pleiadians, another prominent group, are known for their nurturing energy and emphasis on love and community. They are often seen as emissaries of peace, urging humanity to embrace cooperation and harmony. Then there are the Sirians, who hold vast technological knowledge, supporting our understanding of the universe's mysteries and the hidden laws of physics. Each species within the confederation exists to assist humanity, facilitating our awakening and promoting intergalactic unity. Understanding these beings and their specific roles can enhance our connection with them and deepen our interactions as we seek to summon the energies of the Galactic Confederation.

In your quest to connect with these ethereal beings, consider creating a sacred space where you can meditate and raise your vibrational frequency. Visualization can be a powerful tool; imagine inviting beings of light into your space and surrounding yourself with their love and energy. The more open and inviting you are, the more likely you'll attract their presence in your life.

2.2 The Mission of the Galactic Federation

The Galactic Federation holds a profound vision for Earth and humanity, striving to elevate our planet into a new era of cooperation and enlightenment. Their primary goals revolve around fostering a harmonious existence, promoting sustainable practices, and enhancing our consciousness. They see Earth as a pivotal point in the cosmos, a gateway where myriad species and cultures converge. The Federation aims to guide us as we awaken to our true potential, encouraging individuals to explore the depths of their spirituality and connectivity with the universe. They want to help humanity realize that we are not isolated in our struggles but part of a much larger cosmic family, united by shared aspirations for peace and growth.

Unity and peace are cornerstones of the Galactic Federation's mission. They recognize that only through collaboration can we overcome the challenges facing our planet. The Federation sends a clear message: divisions based on nationality, race, or belief systems weaken our collective power. By embracing our differences and working toward common goals, we not only strengthen our communities but also create a vibrant tapestry of cultures that enriches our global experience. This call for unity is not just an ideal; it's a practical approach to building a peaceful future. They emphasize the importance of dialogue, understanding, and compassion, urging us to build bridges rather than walls. In this way, the Federation encourages us to validate one another's experiences and learn from each other's journeys.

To align with the Galactic Federation's mission, consider adopting practices that promote peace and unity in your everyday life. Simple actions like engaging in community service, participating in local dialogues about important social issues, and nurturing respectful relationships can create ripples of positive energy. These efforts not only help to ground your own vibration but also set a powerful example for others. By embodying the principles of peace and cooperation, you contribute to the greater cosmic mission of the Galactic Federation to uplift humanity, making it a more viable partner within the vast, interconnected universe.

2.3 The Frequency of Love and Light

The energetic vibrations of love and light are universal forces that permeate every aspect of existence. These frequencies resonate at a level that is deeply connected to our essence, fostering a sense of unity and compassion. When I first tuned into these energies, I felt as if a warm blanket had wrapped around my spirit, providing solace during tumultuous times. Love and light pulse through the cosmos like the heartbeat of the universe, a gentle reminder that we are all interrelated. They invite us to align with higher states of consciousness, where fear and negativity dissipate, allowing our true selves to shine through. It became clear to me that bringing love and light into my daily life wasn't merely an abstract concept; it is a vital practice that enhances our connection to the universe and our place within it.

Connecting with these frequencies can be a transformative experience that significantly improves our well-being. I remember a night when I sat under a vast, starry sky, meditating on the energy of love and light. As I focused my thoughts on these vibrations, it felt like I was inviting higher consciousness into my being. My worries began to dissolve, and a profound peace filled my heart. This experience heightened not only my sense of joy but also my perception of reality. I started to notice synchronicities appearing in my life—unexpected encounters, guidance from the universe, and a deepened intuition. These moments reminded me that we are never truly alone. Instead, we are cradled in a web of love and light that supports our journey, enhancing our connections with both ourselves and fellow beings. By embracing these frequencies, we can elevate our consciousness and open ourselves up to the wonders of the universe—perhaps even summon the incredible presence of UFOs and the Galactic Confederation of Light.

To cultivate this connection in everyday life, consider incorporating simple practices such as visualization or affirmation. Create moments where you consciously align with the frequency of love and light—whether it's during meditation or simply taking a moment to appreciate the beauty in the world around you. Allow your heart to speak, letting gratitude and compassion flow through you. Remember, the more you resonate with these energies, the more they will manifest in your life, guiding you toward experiences that reflect the love and light you embody.

Chapter 3: Preparing for Contact

3.1 The Importance of Mental Clarity

A clear mind is crucial for facilitating lucid experiences during contact. When I first began my journey into reaching out to UFOs and the Galactic Confederation of Light, I realized that the state of my mind would directly influence the outcomes of my attempts. Mental clarity acts like a finely-tuned receiver, allowing me to perceive signals and energies that might otherwise go unnoticed. With distractions clouding my thoughts, I found it difficult to connect on the deeper levels needed for effective communication. Each time I managed to achieve that clarity, I experienced moments that felt more vivid, more real, and infinitely more profound. It's during those times that I felt an undeniable presence and established a palpable connection with beings of higher consciousness.

To achieve that much-needed mental clarity, I turned to techniques that help center my mind and spirit. Mindfulness has been a game changer for me; it is the practice of tuning into the present moment without judgment. By focusing on my breath and observing my thoughts as they come and go, I could let go of unnecessary worry and anxiety. Meditation, too, has played a pivotal role. I often dedicate time to sit in silence, allowing my thoughts to settle like dust in a still room. I visualize healing white light enveloping me, cleansing away layers of mental clutter. These practices have enabled me to create a sacred space within myself, one where I could cultivate the stillness required to connect with the cosmos.

As you explore the realms of UFOs and higher beings, consider integrating these techniques into your routine. Carving out moments of stillness can unlock pathways to experiences you've yet to discover. Even a few minutes of focused breathing or visualizing a place of peace can help clear the fog from your mind, enhancing your ability to connect with higher vibrational entities. Experiment and see what resonates with you; the key is to create an environment in which your intuition can flow freely. The clearer your mind, the more profound your experiences will be.

3.2 Creating a Sanctuary for Connection

Designing a physical and spiritual space for connecting with the galactic energies requires careful consideration of many elements. Start by choosing a location that feels sacred to you, whether it's in your home, a garden, or a tranquil spot in nature. This space should inspire peace and openness, allowing your spirit to soar. Consider the direction of the place. Some say that opening yourself to the east, where the sun rises, invites new beginnings and possibilities. Surround yourself with objects that hold significance, like crystals that resonate with high frequencies, or images of beings and symbols that inspire you. Soft lighting, gentle colors, and serene sounds play a huge role in setting the mood. I often use quiet music or the sounds of water to enhance this atmosphere. Nature can also be a great source of energy, so if possible, including plants or even a small water feature can help bring the vitality of the earth into your sanctuary.

Creating my own sacred space was a transformative journey. I remember the day I decided to set aside a corner of my living room just for this purpose. It was cluttered with random items, but I cleared everything out, making room for my meditation cushions and a beautiful tapestry that called to me. I added crystals that I felt drawn to, including an amethyst for tranquility and a clear quartz to amplify my intentions. Each piece needed to resonate with my heart, and as I placed them, I felt the energy shift. It was in this space that I first experienced a profound sense of connection, one that felt like an open doorway to the cosmos. I often lit candles and surrounded myself with the scent of sandalwood incense, which seemed to elevate the frequency in the room. This simple act of creating a visual and sensory retreat paved the way for what would become incredible experiences of communion with higher realms.

Every interaction in this sacred space deepened my understanding of the energetics ensuring that where you choose to connect is vital for establishing clear communication. It's about crafting an atmosphere where you feel safe and free to express your deepest thoughts. I encourage you to allow your intuition to guide you in selecting items and aligning arrangements; if something feels right, it probably is. A practical tip would be to perform a small ritual or intention-setting exercise each time you sit in your space. This could be as simple as lighting a candle and stating your intention to connect, or visualizing a beam of light extending toward the stars. Let these rituals reinforce your connection and enhance the sanctity of your enviroment, bridging the gap to the higher realms that are eager to communicate with you.

3.3 Techniques for Heightened Awareness

Exploring practices that enhance our sensory perceptions and awareness opens up a profound realm of possibilities. Engaging with the world through our senses can help us perceive the subtleties that often evade our attention. There are various techniques that have proven to enrich our sensory experiences. Mindfulness meditation allows us to quiet the mind and hone our focus on the present moment, helping us tap into the sights, sounds, and feelings around us. I often find that simply breathing deeply while outdoors increases my awareness of the surrounding environment. The scent of damp earth, the rustle of leaves, and the call of distant birds become amplified, creating a symphony of sensory data that invites deeper connection to not just Earth, but the universe at large. Additionally, techniques like sensory deprivation—immersing oneself in silence or darkness—have been found to sharpen vision or hearing when reintroducing stimuli. These practices create a gateway for intuitive insights and connections that may pulse beyond our immediate reality.

My journey with these techniques has led to numerous interdimensional connections that I often struggle to articulate. During one particularly profound experience, I decided to combine meditation with stargazing. Lying on the grass under a clear night sky, I focused on one bright star that seemed to shimmer with an unusual intensity. As I let my mind drift, I allowed my senses to engage with the cosmos—the chill of the grass against my skin, the vast coolness of the night air, and the rhythmic beating of my heart. Suddenly, subtle whispers of energy enveloped me, guiding me to expand my consciousness. To my astonishment, I began to feel distinct vibrations, a resonance that felt like a conversation with unseen entities from the Galactic Confederation of Light. It was as if my heightened awareness unlocked a portal, allowing me to feel their presence and wisdom through the energy surrounding me. That experience solidified my belief in the power of enhanced awareness as a bridge to the cosmos.

In continuing this journey, a practical tip that has profoundly assisted me is to maintain a journal of sensory experiences. Each time I engage with these techniques, I write down everything I felt, saw, and sensed. Over time, this journal has become a treasure trove of insights and connections, revealing patterns that I might have otherwise overlooked. By documenting these experiences, I not only deepen my practice but also cultivate a deeper understanding of how my sensory perceptions intertwine with the universe. This simple act keeps the spark of curiosity alive and invites further exploration of the cosmic realm.

Chapter 4: Tools for Summoning

4.1 Crystals and Their Energetic Properties

Crystals have an innate ability to amplify energy and facilitate communication, making them vital tools in my practices. Each type of crystal has unique properties that resonate with different vibrational frequencies. For instance, amethyst is often celebrated for its calming energy, which can create a serene space for connecting with higher realms. It's like this soft blanket of energy that wraps around you, allowing you to focus on your intentions without the noise of everyday life. Other crystals, such as clear quartz, can enhance and intensify these energies, acting as a powerful conduit for both sending and receiving messages from beyond. The beauty lies in their diversity; whether it's the warm, grounding energy of hematite or the uplifting frequency of citrine, they all play a role in shaping our experiences and enhancing our communication with the universe.

My personal journey with summoning practices has been deeply intertwined with my choice of crystals. I have experimented with various stones, and each one has offered me a different perspective and outcome. During a particularly powerful session, I placed a selenite wand near me, creating a direct line to the energy I was trying to channel. It felt as if the wand was a beacon, drawing in celestial energies that were eager to communicate. I also have a strong affinity for lapis lazuli, which encourages wisdom and helps enhance psychic abilities. When I work with it, I often find that the messages I receive are clearer and more insightful. Each crystal I use carries its own story, and I believe that our personal experiences with them can open doors to profound understanding and connection with the galactic confederation of light.

It's fascinating how these energetic properties can shift the atmosphere around us. One practical tip I can offer is to create a sacred space where you can connect with these crystals. Set an intention for your practice, hold your chosen crystal, and let the energy flow, allowing yourself to become receptive to the frequencies around you. The more you engage with these stones, the more attuned you become to their energies, slowly revealing the deeper layers of communication waiting to be explored.

4.2 Sound Frequencies and Chanting

Sound vibrations have a profound ability to connect us with the higher realms of existence. When I first discovered how chanting resonated deeply with my being, it was as if a door opened to a dimension previously veiled from my senses. Each sound carries its own frequency, and as we vocalize these tones, we align ourselves with energies that can transcend our earthly experience. The vibrations permeate our environment, creating a bridge between our individual consciousness and the collective consciousness of the universe. Through experimentation, I found that certain chants, when intoned with intention and feeling, can invite higher frequencies to not only surround us but also communicate with us. This connection often manifests as heightened intuition, synchronicities, or even sightings of unidentified flying objects. The practice of sound and vibration awakens dormant parts of our spirit, drawing us closer to the cosmic dance of existence.

Among the chants and frequencies that have personally yielded remarkable results are the ancient mantras and specific tones that seem to resonate with higher extraterrestrial beings. I've had transformative experiences with the "Om" chant, which is said to embody the essence of the universe itself. When I chant "Om" under a starlit sky, I feel a profound sense of unity with all creation, and often I find myself making contact with energies I believe are from the Galactic Confederation of Light. Additionally, I've experimented with the Solfeggio frequencies, particularly the 528 Hz frequency known for its transformational and healing properties. Whenever I immerse myself in chanting at this frequency, I feel my heart expand, and it often coincides with moments of contact or heightened awareness of my surroundings.

A practical way to harness the power of sound is to create a sacred space for your practice. Find a quiet area where you feel safe, and set the mood with candles or soft lighting. When you chant, focus not just on the sound, but on the intention behind your words. Visualize the energies you wish to connect with and allow the vibrations to flow through you. Regular practice creates a resonance that can attract higher dimensional beings. Keep a journal to document your experiences, and you'll probably find that the more you engage with sound and intention, the more your connection to these higher realms deepens. Try experimenting with different chants and frequencies to discover which resonates with you the most.

4.3 Creating a Cosmic Altar

Building a cosmic altar starts with a clear intention. I remember the first time I decided to create one. I found a quiet space in my home, ideally away from distractions, yet close enough to a window that opens to the night sky. This space became my sanctuary, a little world of my own where I felt connected to the universe. The first step was choosing a surface. A small table or even a wooden board can work wonders. I cleaned the area, both physically and energetically, placing my palms on the surface and visualizing any negativity dissolving away.

Next came the components of the altar. I chose items that resonated with me – crystals to amplify the energies, small candles for light, and symbols that represented my intentions, like a tiny model of a UFO or colorful drawings of beings from higher dimensions. Each item was carefully selected. As I arranged them, I focused on the energy they brought. Over time, I learned that incorporating elements of nature, such as feathers or stones collected during my travels, deepened my connection. It felt as if these items were gateways, inviting cosmic visitors to my space.

Once my altar was visually set, I performed a simple ritual. I lit the candles, closed my eyes, and spoke aloud my intentions for contact. This sacred act signified my openness to the universe's messages. I often found that when I spoke my desires openly, holding my hands above the altar, a wave of peace would envelop me, reinforcing my commitment to connecting with the Galactic Confederation of Light.

The energy of a cosmic altar isn't just in its physical components but in the personal meaning we attach to them. When I introduced personal touches, I noticed that my experiences deepened. For instance, I placed a photograph of a moment where I felt particularly connected to the stars—perhaps during a meteor shower or a night at a stargazing event. Every time I glanced at it, I was reminded of that feeling, which amplified the energy of my altar.

Adding colors that resonate with you can also enhance the altar's energy. I often incorporated purples and blues, shades that evoke peace and expansive thinking. The scents of essential oils like frankincense and sandalwood filled the air, creating a sacred atmosphere. I discovered that these aromas helped ground me, making it easier to focus on higher frequencies and prepare for contact with extraterrestrial beings.

It's also essential to maintain and refresh the altar regularly. A simple cleansing ritual, like moving items or adding new elements, can keep the energy vibrant. A thoughtful gesture, such as writing a letter to the universe about my hopes or dreams and placing it on my altar, served as an expression of my ongoing dialogue with the cosmos. Each time I returned to my altar, I felt as if I was stepping into a space where the boundaries between the earthly and the cosmic blurred, continually inviting the galactic energies closer.

Consider allowing your intuition to guide you in how you build and maintain your cosmic altar. Whether you stay consistent with your setup or decide to change things frequently, what matters most is the energy of love and openness that flows from your heart.

Chapter 5: Meditation Techniques for Cosmic Connection

5.1 Guided Meditations for Contact

Exploring the vast universe beyond our understanding has always ignited a spark in my soul. Through various guided meditations, I discovered a pathway to foster a deeper connection with the celestial beings I seek. Each meditation serves as a unique doorway, inviting me to transcend earthly limitations and tap into the divine energies that surround us. One meditation that truly resonates with me involves visualizing a radiant beam of light connecting me with the Galactic Confederation of Light. As I close my eyes, I picture a warm, golden light enveloping my body, filling me with peace and clarity. This visualization helps me tune into the frequencies of love and unity that these beings embody, creating a strong channel of communication between us. The guided voice gently leads me to affirm my intention, emphasizing that I am ready to receive messages and insights from the cosmos. The collective energy of like-minded individuals participating in this meditation amplifies the experience, creating a magnetic field of connection that feels both profound and transformative.

One particular guided meditation stands out in my memory because of the powerful effects it had on my experiences. This meditation, which I prefer to do during quiet evenings under the stars, begins with a soulful invocation to the Pleiadians. As I enter this serene state, I imagine their ship, a brilliant, luminescent vessel, hovering above me, radiating wisdom and love. I have felt an overwhelming sense of belonging during this practice, as if I've touched upon something ancient and sacred. The gentle instructions guide my breath, syncing with the rhythm of the cosmos. I often find myself encountering vivid imagery of intergalactic landscapes, feeling as though I am exploring new realms. After each session, my dreams transform into vivid encounters filled with symbols and messages that challenge me to grow. I can't help but feel that these meditations have opened an intuitive channel, allowing me to receive profound insights and connect with beings beyond my imagination.

To deepen your own experiences, consider creating a dedicated space for these meditations. Whether it's a quiet room or a peaceful corner in nature, your environment enhances the connection. Think about what makes you feel at ease—perhaps some crystals or calming scents to set the mood. Formulate an intention before you meditate, focusing on what you wish to explore or understand. This clarity can help you connect more deeply with the energies around you. Every journey is unique, so allow yourself to be open to whatever emerges during your meditative practice, and trust that the cosmos is always communicating with you.

5.2 Visualization Techniques for Summoning

Visualizing is not just about daydreaming; it's a profound technique that can open doors to the unseen. When I first began exploring the realm of summoning, I quickly learned that the power of intention combined with visualization could create a magnetic pull, inviting energies, entities, and, yes, even UFOs into my experience. By formulating distinct images in my mind, whether it was a shimmering light in the night sky or the hum of a spacecraft, I discovered that these mental pictures acted like beacons, resonating with frequencies that aligned with the Galactic Confederation of Light. This practice cleared the mental clutter and focused my energy towards what I truly desired. The act of visualizing became my way of speaking to the universe—an invitation that often resulted in extraordinary encounters.

One visualization practice that I cherish involves creating a clear and detailed picture of what I wish to see. I find a quiet space, preferably under the stars, and I close my eyes. In my mind's eye, I imagine an open field, bathed in moonlight, where a spaceship suddenly descends; I feel the anticipation in my body and visualize the ship's light illuminating everything around it. This practice is not simply a fantasy; it awakens my senses and synchronizes my energy with higher vibrations. Another technique that has consistently yielded results is the use of guided meditations specifically tailored for summoning. These meditations often incorporate elements of light, love, and cosmic connection, reinforcing my intent while inviting the presence of benevolent beings. During such sessions, I've often felt a rush of energy or even witnessed ethereal lights in the sky shortly after I finish. My personal favorite is also integrating breathwork while visualizing. Deep, intentional breaths allow me to ground my energy and connect with the universe, amplifying my intent as I envision my connection to extraterrestrial realms. Regularly practicing these visualization techniques has not only enhanced my awareness of UFO sightings but has also deepened my connection to the Galactic Confederation of Light.

One useful tip is to create a dedicated visualization space where you feel safe and aligned with your purpose. This could be a corner of your room, a natural setting, or a sacred space where you regularly practice. By doing this, you'll not only reinforce your commitment but also develop a deeper resonance with the energies you wish to attract.

5.3 Breathwork to Raise Your Vibration

Breathwork is a profound practice known for its ability to elevate an individual's energetic frequency. By focusing on our breath, we can connect to deeper aspects of ourselves and the universe. I've personally experienced how various techniques have shifted my vibration and allowed me to align more closely with the energies of the galactic confederation of light. One of the most effective methods I've found is conscious breathing, where you pay attention to the rhythm and quality of your breath, inhaling deeply and exhaling fully. This practice not only calms the mind but also allows for a greater flow of life energy, helping us resonate with higher frequencies. Another technique I've come to love is the circular breathing method, which encourages a continuous flow of breath, creating a loop that fosters a deeper meditative state. In this state, I've felt a resonance with the vibrations of entities that are aligned with love and light. Tuning into these vibrations can facilitate communication with higher realms, opening pathways to understanding the nature of our existence and our connection to cosmic energies.

My journey with breathwork has been nothing short of transformative. Each practice has allowed me to tap into a reservoir of healing energy that feels like a cosmic embrace. One particularly memorable session involved a deep dive into visualizations while performing rhythmic breathing. As I breathed in, I envisioned golden light enveloping me, pulling in the energies of uplifting beings. On the exhale, I released anything that felt heavy or dark, creating space for the light. The more I practiced, the clearer my connection became to the galactic confederation of light. I began to receive messages; whispers of encouragement that I was on the right path. I also experimented with different postures during breathwork. Sitting up straight while placing my hands on my heart center allowed me to amplify the energetic vibration in my body. This simple act dramatically enhanced the frequency of my breath, enabling me to feel connected to a greater cosmic unity. Remembering to set intentions before starting a breathwork session can act like a cosmic compass, guiding your experience. This subtle practice of intention setting combined with the breath creates an ethereal space where miracles can occur.

For anyone looking to elevate their energetic frequency, I encourage you to experiment with these breathwork techniques. The journey is as important as the destination. Take the time to create a sacred space for yourself during these practices. Trust your intuition to guide you in exploring the beautiful relationship between breath and cosmic energy.

Chapter 6: Signs of Galactic Presence

6.1 Understanding Unexplained Phenomena

Throughout our very human journey, there have been countless unexplained occurrences that seem to point to something greater than ourselves. I have always been captivated by the idea that there are forces at play in our universe that we cannot fully comprehend. From eerie lights flickering in the night sky to strange sounds resonating from nowhere, these phenomena can feel like breadcrumbs leading us toward a galactic presence. Often, these experiences defy logic and challenge our understanding of reality. I've witnessed the shimmering glow of unexplained orbs dancing silently above me, captivating my gaze and igniting an insatiable curiosity within. The more I delve into these occurrences, the more I realize they can be potential signals from civilizations far beyond our own, hinting at the existence of the galactic confederation of light. Listening carefully to these signals, whether in the form of unusual sightings or inexplicable changes in our environment, can open the door to understanding our place in a vastly interconnected universe.

Personal stories often carry a weight that transcends a mere account of events; they can illuminate the path toward recognition of our cosmic connections. I recall one evening, standing in an open field, looking up at the velvet expanse of stars. Suddenly, I spotted an unusual craft—gliding silently, emitting a pulsating luminescence. My heart raced as I felt an undeniable connection to a realm of existence that was just out of reach. Others share similar anecdotes; friends have described instances of encountering strange beings, or experiencing vivid dreams laden with messages that seemed to speak directly to their souls. These bizarre experiences often linger long after they occur. They serve as reminders that we might not be alone, that glimpses of extraterrestrial life can pour into our consciousness in inexplicable ways, nudging us toward a deeper understanding of the universe and our role within it.

As you seek to connect with these unexplained phenomena yourself, it's vital to remain open-hearted and curious. Create space in your life for quiet observation. Sometimes, the universe speaks in whispers; observing the stars, meditating, or spending quiet time in nature allows those whispers to take form. Keep a journal to document any unusual experiences or feelings that arise, as they could act as a guide in your journey toward galactic understanding and connection.

6.2 Messages Received Through Synchronicities

Synchronicity is a fascinating concept that speaks to the idea of meaningful coincidences. It's not just random chance when events align in ways that feel significant; rather, it can be viewed as a form of communication from the universe. In my journey of summoning UFOs and connecting with the Galactic Confederation of Light, I have found that these synchronicities serve as guiding lights, revealing messages that are often subtle yet profoundly impactful. The universe communicates with us in a language of symbols and aligned happenings, which can sometimes lead us to answers we're seeking or push us toward our intended paths.

During my summoning journey, I began to recognize the key synchronicities that accompanied my efforts. There were moments that felt too perfectly timed to be mere coincidence. For example, when I encountered specific numbers repeatedly or had unexpected meetings with individuals who shared insights about the stars, it felt as if the universe were sending me messages about my purpose. One particularly powerful experience involved witnessing a flock of birds flying in a formation that mirrored the shape of a UFO. At that moment, I understood that such events were not just happening; they were affirmations of my connection to something greater. Each synchronicity deepened my understanding and brought me closer to the realities of interdimensional contact.

As you journey your own path, remain open to the signs around you. Pay attention to the thoughts that cross your mind during these instances, and take note of feelings or inspirations you receive. Keeping a journal can help track these occurrences and reveal patterns over time. The more you recognize these synchronicities, the more attuned you will become to the universe's whispers guiding your summoning practice. Always remember, the universe has a way of communicating; it's up to us to listen and interpret the messages shared with us.

6.3 The Language of Light Codes

Light codes serve as a profound and intricate form of communication from higher realms. Often, these are perceived as radiant symbols, colors, or frequencies that carry specific meanings. Each code seems to resonate with a particular vibration, crafted by advanced civilizations and spiritual beings who wish to share wisdom and guidance. As I delved deeper into my journey of understanding these light codes, I realized that they are not mere visuals but rather a language that speaks directly to our souls. The more I opened myself up to experiencing these codes, the clearer their messages became, revealing an expansive network of communication that transcends our ordinary perception. There's a palpable energy that comes with the codes, inviting us to remember our connectedness to cosmic consciousness and the universe itself.

My personal experiences with interpreting light codes have transformed my understanding of communication with the universe. I recall one evening, as the sun dipped below the horizon, I was drawn outdoors. I stood in a clearing, embraced by the cool breeze and a sky dotted with stars, when suddenly, I began to see swirling patterns of light. These patterns danced before my eyes, almost as if they were alive, and I felt a rush of energy course through me. As I relaxed into the experience, I began to receive messages that transcended words. It was as though the vibrant colors and shifting patterns were inviting me to contemplate my role within the vast cosmos. I began to intuitively decode the feelings accompanying each light hue, each twinkling twirl of illumination—some spoke of love and healing, others of guidance and truth. This intuitive connection helped me refine my understanding, allowing me to interpret these light codes as a universal language that resonates on a soul level.

Engaging with light codes requires an open heart and a willingness to explore beyond the limitations of traditional communication. During meditative practices or even during moments of quiet reflection, I've found these codes can be activated, revealing insights that can guide decision-making or enhance personal growth. To foster this connection, it can be helpful to focus on your breath, clear your mind, and simply allow the images to come to you. Embrace whatever you visualize, no matter how abstract or unclear. Sometimes, it might even feel like a gentle whisper in your heart, encouraging you to trust in the messages received. The more you practice, the more vivid and cogent these light codes will become, helping you to truly connect with the galactic confederation of light. Embrace your journey into this radiant language of the universe, for within it lies not only cosmic knowledge but a beautiful confirmation of our interconnectedness with all that exists.

Chapter 7: Safe Practices in Summoning

7.1 Grounding Techniques After Contact

After a contact experience, whether it was a visual encounter or an intuitive communication with beings from the Galactic Confederation of Light, one might find themselves feeling a bit unanchored. Grounding oneself quickly becomes an essential practice to regain balance and harmony. One method I often use is to focus on my breath. By taking deep, deliberate breaths, I can feel my feet connecting with the ground beneath me. The simple act of inhaling deeply through the nose and exhaling slowly through the mouth helps to clear my mind and focus my energy back into my physical body. This not only helps realign my thoughts but also brings a sense of calm, as each breath fills me with reassurance and stillness.

Another effective technique involves visualizing roots extending from my feet deep into the Earth. This image strengthens my connection to the planet and promotes feelings of stability and safety. I often imagine these roots drawing up energy from the Earth, filling me with warmth and grounding myself further. Following visualizations, I find it beneficial to engage my senses by paying attention to my surroundings. I focus on the colors, sounds, and textures that envelop me, which assists in redirecting my attention away from any disorienting energy leftover from my encounter.

Sharing grounding techniques is essential, and I've come to find a few that resonate strongly with myself and others after contact experiences. One particular method involves carrying crystals with me. Rose quartz or black tourmaline can serve as protective stones that help to transmute energy and keep me centered. Whenever I hold these crystals in my hand or place them in my pocket, I feel a sense of connection and protection. Additionally, performing light stretching or yoga immediately after contact can reinvigorate both the body and mind, helping to release any tension that may have accumulated. Remember, each experience is unique, so find what feels right for you, and don't hesitate to try new techniques until you discover the ones that bring you a sense of tranquility and grounding.

7.2 Protecting Your Energy Field

Every time I step outside and feel the light breeze on my skin, I'm reminded of how important it is to protect my energy field from potential negative influences. I have encountered many situations where my energy felt drained or restricted due to the presence of others or the environments I found myself in. One of the most effective ways I've learned to safeguard my energy is through conscious awareness and intention. By simply being mindful of the people I surround myself with, I can sense if their energy is uplifting or depleting. I've noticed that taking a moment to ground myself before entering crowded spaces helps maintain my energy. Grounding involves visualizing roots extending from my feet into the Earth, enabling me to draw up stabilizing energy that buffers me against external negativity. Additionally, embracing crystals has proven to be a powerful ally. Carrying stones like black tourmaline or selenite not only adds a layer of protection but also aids in dispelling any lingering negative energies that I may encounter throughout my day.

Engaging in rituals reinforces my auric field in profoundly comforting ways. I've developed a daily practice that includes meditating each morning while envisioning a golden light enveloping me. This light serves as a protective shield against unwanted intrusions. I often recite affirmations during this time, affirming that only positive and loving energies may approach me. Creating sacred space is also vital; I always keep a designated area in my home where I can retreat, surrounded by items that resonate with high vibrational energy, such as meaningful crystals, plants, and images of my galactic guides. My environment reflects the protection I wish to cultivate, so I frequently cleanse this space through smoke from sage or palo santo, allowing any negativity to dissipate. Taking moments throughout the day to visualize a bubble of light surrounding me has also helped maintain my energy integrity, acting as a barrier that filters out negativity while inviting positive energies to thrive.

In this journey, I've discovered the importance of balance. While it's vital to protect our energy, it's equally crucial to remain open to the joy and love the universe offers. By integrating practices like gratitude and mindfulness into my daily life, I find that I can navigate both light and darker energies with grace. A simple tip I've adopted is to close my eyes and take a few deep breaths whenever I feel overwhelmed. Imagining a refreshing wave of light washing over me helps reset my energy. This powerful technique can be done anywhere and serves to remind me that I am in control of my energy field, helping me stay aligned with my purpose as I connect with the higher realms, including the magnificent beings from the galactic confederation of light.

7.3 Setting Intentions for Positive Connections

Setting clear, positive intentions is fundamental to creating a meaningful connection when summoning. Intentions act as a powerful beacon, guiding energies towards us and shaping the experiences we attract. When I first started my journey in exploring the realms of UFOs and the Galactic Confederation of Light, I quickly realized that my mindset was crucial. Just as a lighthouse guides ships through the fog, my intentions helped illuminate my path. Instead of simply desiring contact, I began to ask myself what I truly wanted from these interactions. Was it knowledge, healing, or perhaps a sense of belonging? By clarifying my desires and aligning them with positive intentions, I harnessed a greater potential to connect with higher energies. It's like tuning a radio to the right frequency; clear intentions help tune into the right vibrational match.

As I progressed, I had experiences that reinforced the power behind well-crafted intentions. I remember one particular evening when I felt the urge to connect more deeply. Instead of expressing vague wishes, I sat in quiet reflection, focusing on what I genuinely wanted to achieve through this connection. I articulated my intention: "I seek understanding and companionship." The moment I set this intention, I felt an immediate shift in energy around me. It was as if the universe had taken notice, responding to my heartfelt calling. After a few moments, I felt a presence I hadn't sensed before. This experience underscored how essential clarity and positivity are in my approach. Friends and fellow seekers often ask me for tips, and I always stress the importance of crafting intentions with care. They shouldn't just be scripts we recite but heartfelt expressions of our desires. The more sincere and focused they are, the more powerful the connection that can follow. This alignment often extends beyond just UFOs; it seeps into daily life, creating opportunities for relationships and experiences that fulfill and enrich. I encourage anyone looking to deepen their connection with the cosmos to spend time in reflection. What is it that you genuinely seek? Write it down, speak it aloud, and let that energy resonate into the universe.

Remember, clarity is key, but positivity amplifies your reach. By embracing a mindset that is not only clear but also filled with gratitude, love, and hope, you open yourself up to a universe filled with endless possibilities. Each time you set an intention, visualize it enveloped in a warm glow, feeling the joy that accompanies the realization of your desires. This practice of setting intentions is not merely a formality; it transforms the way we engage with the world and the cosmic forces that surround us. So, take a moment each day to connect with your heart, express your intentions clearly, and watch as the pathways to extraordinary connections unfold before you.

Chapter 8: The Role of Intention

8.1 Aligning Your Intent with Universal Energy

Our intentions are powerful forces that shape the reality we experience. When I first began delving into the world of summoning UFOs and connecting with the galactic confederation of light, I quickly realized how crucial it was to understand the impact of my thoughts and desires. Intentions are not just thoughts; they are energetic blueprints that resonate with the universe. Each time I focused on an intention, I felt a shift in my energy, as if the universe was echoing my desires back to me.

Every intention carries a vibrational frequency. For instance, the intention to connect with higher beings comes with a different energy signature compared to a more grounded desire like finding a parking space. It's essential to cultivate clarity in our thoughts, for confusion leads to mixed signals being sent out into the cosmos. I remember the first time I truly grasped this concept; I was standing outside under a starlit sky, feeling the vastness around me. I closed my eyes and envisioned a connection with higher dimensions, and in that moment, I felt the energy shift. It was as if the entire universe was attuning to my clarity and openness.

Aligning my intentions with universal energies has been a transformative journey. I've discovered that the key is not just in the desire to connect with extraterrestrial beings but in preparing myself energetically. I began practicing meditation regularly, allowing quiet moments to clear my mind and foster an open channel. This practice created a fertile ground for my intentions to take root. Through quiet reflection, I learned to listen to the nuances of my energy, understanding when I was truly aligned versus when I was distracted or disconnected.

One powerful experience that stands out took place during a particularly quiet night. I had set a clear intention to welcome communication from the galactic confederation. Instead of rushing into the summoning, I first focused on raising my vibration through gratitude and love. I visualized a light surrounding me, inviting positive energies to come forth. The result was not immediate, but as I tuned into the subtle energies, I noticed changes in my surroundings. Lights flickered, and my heart raced with excitement, providing undeniable proof that aligning with universal energies was indeed possible. A crucial takeaway from this is to remember that our intentions, when amplified with genuine energy and purpose, create a pathway to the extraordinary. Each moment of clarity brings us closer to making contact with those we seek.

To effectively harness your intentions, consider establishing a regular practice of grounding and cleansing your energy. Simple methods like spending time in nature, practicing mindful breathing, or engaging in joyful activities can significantly elevate your energetic frequency. This alignment can help pave the way for profound experiences in your journey of summoning and connection.

8.2 Creating a Collective Intention Group

When we gather as a group with a unified intention, something remarkable happens. There's an amplification of energy that can truly change the dynamics of our manifesting process. It's as if our collective consciousness harmonizes, creating a resonance that draws in what we seek, whether it's a connection with extraterrestrial beings or the opportunity to experience their guidance. In my experience, the synergy of minds locked in a mutual aim can sharpen our focus and elevate our energies far beyond what we can achieve alone. When everyone is aligned with the same purpose, their individual intent becomes part of a greater whole, resulting in vibrational shifts that are palpable in the air. This collective magnetism becomes a beacon, potentially attracting the very phenomena we wish to summon, like UFO sightings or communications from the Galactic Confederation of Light.

During sessions with my collective intention circles, I have witnessed firsthand the power of shared energies. Everyone brings their unique vibe to the table, and when that's directed towards a singular goal, it feels like the universe listens. The collaborative meditations, focused breathing, and intentional visualizations turn into a dance of energies, intertwining and amplifying each person's desires. I remember the first time we attempted to summon a UFO. Each person shared what they desired to see or experience, and as we concentrated, I could feel the energy in the room shift. It became electric, charged with hope and intention. That night, several of us spotted unusual lights in the sky, and while it wasn't conclusive, it sparked an undeniable sense of connection to something greater.

Establishing a collective intention circle started out as a personal challenge, but it transformed into a beautiful journey of discovery and empowerment. My first step was finding like-minded individuals who shared a passion for exploring the mysteries of the universe. We began gathering weekly, each member contributing their energy and intentions. What I quickly learned was the importance of creating a safe and open environment. Trust and respect were key; it allowed everyone to express their desires authentically without fear of judgment. Each session would begin with grounding exercises that mentally and spiritually prepared us, allowing our intentions to flow harmoniously together.

In one of our circles, we decided to focus specifically on contacting beings from the Galactic Confederation of Light. We set a date, each bringing our personal energy and stories, and we created a sacred space; candles were lit, crystals were placed, and our intentions were written down and shared aloud. As we held hands and focused, I could feel a sense of connection building not just among us, but potentially to the cosmic energies we aimed to reach. After our intense session, we stepped outside and, to our amazement, we saw a cluster of lights forming patterns in the night sky. Although it could have been a coincidence, the feeling that we were part of something larger felt too profound to ignore. Each small success drove our enthusiasm further and deepened our commitment to the practice.

A practical tip for anyone considering forming their own collective intention group is to prioritize the space you create. Ensure it's inviting, calming, and resonates with all members. Encourage open communication, and don't shy away from celebrating small signs or synchronicities that might arise during your sessions. These shared victories reinforce the belief that what you're doing is significant and worthwhile.

8.3 The Power of Clear and Specific Requests

When I first started my journey into connecting with the cosmos, I quickly realized that the clarity and specificity of my requests were paramount. It's not just about wishing for something to happen or throwing vague desires into the universe, but about articulating exactly what I seek. For instance, when I desired a sign of extraterrestrial presence, instead of simply asking for "a UFO to appear," I learned to refine my request. I began asking for a specific type of craft, glowing in a particular color, appearing at a certain time in a particular location. This shift in my approach helped me understand the intricate dance between intention and manifestation. In asking the universe for clear, specific experiences, it became evident that the cosmos responds to the details we provide, making every interaction feel intentional and meaningful.

Reflecting on my experiences, I can remember one extraordinary evening where I made a very specific request to witness a fleet of lightships. Instead of simply hoping for a sighting, I concentrated on the aspects I wanted to see: the shimmering silver light, the pattern in which they would move, and the time of twilight when the horizon would play host to magic. The results were astonishing. As dusk settled, a series of orbs appeared, dancing in the heavens just as I had envisioned. This profound encounter was not merely by chance; it was a direct result of the specific request I had summoned. Through the weeks that followed, I heard many stories from fellow seekers, each echoing the same truth—those who crafted targeted requests experienced more genuine and transformative encounters.

In my practice of engaging with the universe, I've learned a revolutionary technique: writing down my requests. Putting pen to paper brings a sense of permanence and seriousness to my intentions, solidifying them in ways that mere thoughts do not. I suggested this to others within my community, and many reported back that their experiences began to shift dramatically. The act of writing and then vocalizing these requests seems to amplify the energy around them, making it palpable. As you embark on your own journey, remember, clarity is your ally. Be as specific as possible, and enrich your requests with emotional energy and intent. This simple yet profound shift can open doors to cosmic interactions that you never imagined possible.

Chapter 9: Observational Practices for UFO Sightings

9.1 Ideal Locations for Skywatching

Identifying the best spots for observing UFOs often requires tapping into the collective knowledge of communities that share this interest. Locations where people have reported sightings or unexplained phenomena often become hot spots for like-minded individuals eager to connect with the unknown. Engaging with local groups, attending skywatching events, or participating in online forums can provide invaluable insights into where the most active areas are. Often, remote locations away from city lights, such as national parks, mountain overlooks, or open fields, yield the best results. I've found that places with a clear horizon and minimal obstructions offer the perfect panorama for spotting those elusive crafts that many believe are interdimensional or extraterrestrial in nature. A community may refer to specific areas by names passed down through generations, sometimes linked to stories of sightings that echo through time.

As for personal favorite locations, one unforgettable experience occurred on a quiet night atop a mountain ridge in Colorado. The sky seemed to come alive, with twinkling stars swirling across the inky blackness. I remember sitting on a blanket, surrounded by fellow enthusiasts, sharing stories while eagerly scanning the sky. Then it happened—a series of bright orbs danced across our vision, moving in ways that defied the natural laws we understand. Each person around me reacted with a mix of awe and exhilaration, a shared recognition of something extraordinary. Other favorite spots include remote beaches at midnight, where the vast ocean mirrors the starry sky, and desert vistas that stretch endlessly, allowing for uninterrupted stargazing. Each location carries its own energy and history, and those moments spent in the embrace of the cosmos deepen one's connection to the galactic confederation of light.

To maximize your skywatching experiences, prepare yourself by learning about the moon phases and seasonal constellations. Knowing peak times for possible UFO activity, typically during meteor showers or on clear, moonless nights, can greatly enhance your chances of discovery. Bring along comfortable gear, like a reclining chair or a cozy blanket, and perhaps a journal to document your sightings. Share your experiences with others, as each story shared can add to the collective understanding of our place in the universe. Keep your heart open and your mind curious—these two elements may be key to summoning the phenomena you seek.

9.2 The Best Times to Look Up

Timing strategies can greatly enhance the chances of encountering UFOs. Many of us have become keen observers of the night sky, and I have discovered that specific times can yield more sightings than others. The hours around twilight, just after sunset or just before dawn, often seem to elicit more activity. This period of dim light allows our eyes to adjust, and it seems as though the beings from the galactic confederation of light take advantage of this natural transition. Additionally, during meteor showers or when there are notable celestial events such as planetary alignments, the energy in the atmosphere seems to rise. It's as if these events open up gateways that allow higher energies to intersect with our own dimension, increasing the likelihood of UFO interactions. Therefore, marking your calendar for such events could be crucial. When you're out there, patience is essential; sometimes, you might have to look up for hours, but the right moment could happen in the blink of an eye.

Reflecting on my own experiences, I've noticed significant variations during different phases of the moon. When the moon is full, its bright light can illuminate the sky, making it harder to catch the subtle movements of UFOs. However, during the new moon, the absence of lunar light creates a darker canvas for the stars to shine and often seems to attract these craft. My most memorable sightings occurred during new moons; I felt as if the cosmos were whispering secrets to those who were willing to truly listen. Celestial events, like eclipses, have also provided profound moments of connection. During one specific eclipse, the atmosphere felt charged, and my intent to connect was met with a dazzling display of lights dancing in the shadows. The synchronicity of these moments often feels like an invitation from the universe. It reinforces the idea that when we align ourselves with nature's cycles, we not only connect with the stars above but with the essence of the cosmos itself.

As you embark on your journey of UFO summoning, consider practicing under the veil of darkness that new moons provide or during celestial events that spark excitement. To maximize your chances, prepare a small ritual or set your intentions before looking up at the sky. A focused mind and an open heart can make all the difference. Embrace the magic of the universe and remind yourself: Every time you look up, you're opening a door to infinite possibilities.

9.3 Documenting Your Experiences

Documenting my experiences with UFO sightings and encounters has been an essential part of my journey. Keeping a logbook allows me to track not just the physical aspects of what I see, but also the emotions, thoughts, and insights that arise during these encounters. Each sighting is unique, and recording the details helps me to notice patterns over time. I began by noting the date, time, location, weather conditions, and specific descriptions of what I observed. This simple act of writing down the facts has transformed into a treasure trove of memories and revelations.

More than just a record, my logbook serves as a tool for reflection. It documents my growth in understanding the phenomena and my emotional responses. I can revisit the initial wonder I felt during my first sighting, or reflect on how my perceptions have evolved. This practice has fostered a deeper connection with the galactic energies surrounding us. In sharing my logs with others, I've found that this documentation can spark conversations and inspire others to embark on their own journeys, creating a community of like-minded seekers.

To effectively document my experiences, I've developed a systematic approach that I find both fulfilling and enlightening. I dedicate time after each sighting to sit quietly and recount everything I observed. I write down the initial emotions that surged through me; was it excitement, fear, or curiosity? These feelings often hold valuable clues about what the encounter means to me personally. After this initial reflection, I take the time to add sketches or diagrams. Sometimes, simply drawing what I saw helps to cement the experience in my mind. I find that these illustrations bring a vibrant energy to my logbook, making it more than just a collection of notes.

Recording all of these details in a consistent format allows me to look back and identify shifts in my understanding or encounters that might resonate with larger cosmic events. I also make sure to include any synchronistic events related to my sightings, such as significant thoughts I had beforehand or messages I received during meditation. By connecting the dots, I create a cohesive narrative that not only chronicles my journey but also aligns my personal growth with the broader mission of understanding what we are experiencing together. One practical tip is to set aside a few moments after each encounter, no matter how brief, to jot down your immediate thoughts and feelings. This simple discipline can lead to profound insights over time.

Chapter 10: Communicating with the Galactic Federation

10.1 Using Telepathy for Connection

Telepathy is often seen as a mystical ability, yet it embodies a form of communication that resonates with the very essence of human experience. I've come to realize that telepathy isn't just the stuff of sci-fi movies; it's a natural way of connecting with other beings, realms, and dimensions. Many of us possess an innate ability to communicate on levels beyond spoken language. This method, rooted in empathy and intuitive understanding, opens channels between souls, transcending the physical barriers of speech and sound. When I first began exploring this concept, it felt like tapping into an ancient wisdom long overlooked. It became clear that our thoughts and feelings carry vibrations that can resonate with others, facilitating a connection that might initially appear supernatural. As we delve deeper into our consciousness, we recognize that telepathy is like tuning into a universal frequency where thoughts and emotions meld into pure understanding.

The real magic of telepathy is its capability to foster profound connections with beings, both terrestrial and extraterrestrial. There are moments when I found myself reaching out mentally, particularly during meditative states or moments of deep focus under the night sky. In these instances, I felt a sense of unity, as if my intentions were sending waves through the cosmos, inviting responses from the unknown. The very act of quieting the mind and tuning into these frequencies made me feel like a participant in a grand dialogue—one that linked not just myself to others, but also to the greater universe. My awareness expanded, and I could sense the existence of energies that were not bound by physical forms or limitations of conventional communication.

One transformative experience stands out vividly in my memory, a night punctuated by shooting stars and celestial wonders. As I gazed into the vastness of the sky, I set an intention to connect with the cosmic beings I believed existed beyond our realm. With each moment that passed, I began to quiet my thoughts, allowing space for a conversation to unfold. I closed my eyes and focused on projecting my thoughts about peace and unity into the universe. A sudden warmth enveloped me, as if invisible hands were cradling my intentions softly. Shortly after, I felt a distinct vibration pulsing in sync with my heartbeat, a clear sign that my call had been heard.

A few days later, I had what some might describe as a visitation. I was not asleep, yet I felt transported to an alternate space where the air shimmered with light. It was there that I encountered beings made of light, radiating love and understanding. We weren't speaking in words; instead, I felt emotions conveyed through vivid images and sensations. Their presence brought me clarity—reminders of interconnectedness and the importance of maintaining a loving energy. This experience left me with not just awe, but a deep-seated understanding of telepathy as a channel for connecting with wisdom far greater than myself. The more I practiced reaching out to them through my thoughts, the more I encountered interactions that confirmed I wasn't alone in the universe. I learned that to invite these connections, focusing on love and pure intentions is key.

Embracing telepathy as a way to connect opens doors to extraordinary experiences and relationships that enrich our lives. For those looking to enhance their telepathic abilities, be consistent in asking questions and sharing your thoughts with the universe. Clear your mind, listen attentively, and trust the sensations or insights that come your way. The more you practice, the clearer the messages will become, allowing you to create vibrant connections with those from other realms.

10.2 Journaling Conversations with Beings of Light

Journaling has become a profound practice for me, serving as a bridge to maintain communication with cosmic entities that share insights of a higher frequency. Each time I sit down with my journal, I create a sacred space for the vibrational energies of light beings to connect with me. This practice allows me to document encounters, celestial messages, and intuitive nudges I receive during my meditations or while I'm simply in quiet reflection. It transforms my thoughts and experiences into tangible records—a pathway through which these otherworldly beings can share wisdom and guidance.

What excites me most about journaling in this way is the serendipity of unexpected revelations. Sometimes, I don't even realize I've tapped into a deeper understanding until I revisit those pages. The act of writing feels like a dialogue where I ask questions and the answers flow through my pen. I've learned to trust the process, recognizing the value of these moments when the spirit world collaborates with me. Through this journaling practice, I preserve the essence of these communications, becoming a conduit of higher knowledge that nourishes not only my own spirit but potentially others who may later read my reflections.

In my journaling journey, I have collected snippets that capture the essence of wisdom shared by these light beings. One entry that stands out is from a particularly vibrant evening where I felt an overwhelming presence surrounding me. I scribbled down, "They reminded me that love is the universal language; it transcends all barriers and brings forth a powerful healing energy." This simple yet profound statement resonated deeply with me, underscoring the importance of love in all exchanges—whether with ourselves, our fellow beings on this planet, or those enlightened entities among the stars.

Another excerpt relays a vision I had during a meditation, depicted with vivid clarity in my writing. I noted, "I was guided to a vast, colorful landscape where beings of light danced and laughed. They shared with me the understanding that joy is a frequency to operate from, that our collective happiness elevates humanity." Reflecting on these encounters not only enriches my understanding but serves as a reminder of the joy and unity we can cultivate here on Earth. As I dive back into these snippets, I feel a persistent call to share this information—illuminating the path for others who seek connection with the Galactic Confederation of Light.

Maintaining a journal dedicated to these conversations can be incredibly beneficial. Not only does it empower you to capture fleeting moments of insight, but it also becomes a treasure trove of guidance that you can return to whenever you seek solace or direction in your journey.

10.3 Inviting Positive Entities into Your Space

Creating a welcoming environment for positive entities begins with intention. When I started this journey, I discovered that simply focusing on the desire to connect with benevolent beings can shift the energy in my space. I found it valuable to cleanse my environment first. Burning sage or using sound through singing bowls resonated deeply during my meditative practices. I felt the vibrations uplift the areas around me, creating a vibrant, open pathway for good energy to flow in.

Setting up a dedicated space was key. I chose a corner of my room and adorned it with crystals, candles, and images that carried loving energy. Each element I added resonated personally with me, allowing me to cultivate a sanctuary filled with light. I often utilized colored lights, particularly soft whites and gentle blues, as they felt calming and inviting during my evening meditations. The more I focused on this space, the more I sensed a subtle energy shift, and I began practicing daily affirmations to welcome these celestial beings into my home.

After consistently inviting these benevolent entities, I noticed remarkable changes in my surroundings. My dreams became vibrant, often filled with celestial imagery and profound messages. Each morning, I woke feeling lighter, more centered, and ready to embrace the day. I frequently took walks under the stars, feeling a connection that transcended the physical realm. Those moments became sacred, as I began receiving subtle signs of their presence, whether it was a gentle gust of wind that felt like a loving touch or the sudden appearance of a shooting star.

These experiences have left me in awe. Each time I engaged with meditative rituals and open-hearted prayers, I sensed the gentle comforting energy envelop me, enlightening not only my spirit but also those around me. Friends who visited commented on the peaceful atmosphere, sharing feelings of calm and joy as they stepped into my space. The more I nurtured this inviting environment, the more I felt the connection strengthen, teaching me that simply opening my heart and home to positive entities could yield transformative energy shifts. Regularly expressing gratitude for these encounters has further deepened this inviting relationship, enhancing not only my spiritual journey but enriching my entire life experience. Consider keeping a journal to track your experiences and insights, as it acts as a powerful tool to reflect on the growth you'll witness on this incredible path.

Chapter 11: Astral Travel and Contact

11.1 Preparing for Astral Projection

Preparing for astral projection requires more than just a desire to explore the universe beyond our physical bodies; it demands a calm mind and a receptive spirit. In my experience, the environment plays a crucial role in facilitating this journey. Find a quiet space where you won't be disturbed, dim the lights, and perhaps light some candles or incense to elevate the ambiance. This sensory setting helps signal to your mind that you are entering a sacred space, perfect for exploration.

Relaxation techniques are essential. Deep breathing is a wonderful practice that calms both the mind and the body. As you breathe in slowly, visualize inhaling light and energy, and as you exhale, let go of any tension or stress. This mindful breathing brings your awareness inward, setting the stage for your experience. Consider lying down comfortably, ensuring that your body feels supported. I often find that gentle music or sound frequencies designed for meditation can enhance my state of relaxation. Allow yourself to surrender to the moment, feeling the weight of your body become lighter as your mind drifts away from everyday concerns.

Many people experience fear when they first consider astral projection, and I certainly was no different. This fear often stems from the unknown; the thought of leaving your body can be intimidating. Acknowledging these fears is the first step toward overcoming them. I recommend reminding yourself that you are in control. Visualization techniques can be incredibly powerful here. Imagine yourself surrounded by a protective light or energy bubble, assuring yourself that you are safe throughout your journey. This visualization creates a strong intention that helps to mitigate fear.

Speaking from personal experience, I've learned that journaling about my astral travel intentions and fears can be cathartic. Writing down what worries you can help you process those emotions. I also encourage looking into positive testimonies from others who have successfully experienced astral projection. Hearing about their journeys can give you hope and inspiration, helping to quell any lingering doubts. Embrace the process as a wondrous adventure; focus on the thrilling possibilities that await you rather than the fear of what might happen. Understanding that these experiences are ultimately about exploration and learning can transform your perspective, enriching your journey beyond the stars.

As you prepare for this fascinating journey, remember to set a clear intention for your astral travel. What do you want to explore? What questions do you have for the universe? A clear intention can serve as your guiding star, illuminating the path as you navigate the astral realm.

11.2 Navigating the Astral Realms

Navigating the astral realms requires a blend of intention and protection, as each plane has its own frequency and characteristics. To embark on this journey, I always begin with a grounding technique. I envision roots extending from my feet into the Earth, anchoring me. This connection keeps me stable and allows me to explore without being lost in the vastness of the astral space. When setting out to visit different astral planes, such as the etheric, mental, or celestial, I focus on cultivating a strong sense of purpose. Each plane beckons with its unique attributes—some may offer healing energies, while others could be filled with chaotic vibrations. It's essential to maintain clarity of thought and intention as you traverse these layers. Surrounding myself with light, I envision a bubble of protection that wards off any unwanted energies or entities. By creating this space, I ensure that my exploration remains safe and fulfilling.

Through my own navigational experiences, I've encountered incredible galactic phenomena. One particularly vivid experience occurred when I set my sights on the Pleiades star cluster. As I projected my consciousness there, the vibrant energy of the stars enveloped me. I distinctly felt the warmth and welcoming embrace from beings filled with compassion and wisdom. They communicated with me through light codes, which I understood instinctively, not needing words. This encounter deepened my understanding of their existence and the interconnectedness of all beings. I've also found the experience of summoning UFOs through focused intention to be truly exhilarating. By channeling my energy and joining it with the frequencies of love and light, I've seen orbs appear in the night sky as a response to my call. Each encounter fosters a feeling of unity with the galactic confederation of light and enriches my journey.

11.3 Meeting Galactic Beings in Alternate Dimensions

During my journey through the realms of astral travel, I often find myself contemplating the vastness of the universe and the potential for encounters with extraterrestrial life. There's something exhilarating about leaving my physical body behind and exploring dimensions beyond the constraints of time and space. With focused intention and an open heart, I navigate through these alternate realities, where the energy of different beings vibrates at unique frequencies. The possibilities seem endless, and with each journey, the idea of meeting galactic beings feels increasingly tangible.

Astral travel allows me to tap into higher realms that often feel just a breath away from our earthly existence. As I shift my awareness and let go of earthly attachments, I sense the presence of beings from different star systems. It's about tuning into their frequency, something akin to dialing into a radio station that plays music from another world. Sometimes, I feel a gentle pull, as if invisible threads connect us, drawing me closer to the vibrant energy of extraterrestrial entities. The experience is transformative; I am reminded that the universe is richly populated with life beyond our imagination, just waiting to be acknowledged.

My personal encounters during astral projections have been nothing short of awe-inspiring. On one memorable occasion, as I floated through a brilliant landscape shimmering with colors unseen in this reality, I came across a group of luminous beings. They emanated warmth and love, communicating telepathically rather than through words. I remember being overwhelmed by the sensation of unconditional compassion enveloping me, igniting a deep understanding of connection. Each encounter felt like a homecoming, sparking knowledge about our place in the universe and the collective consciousness.

The experiences recounting these interactions with galactic beings emphasize the profound shifts I've noticed within myself. Many went beyond mere encounters; they were invitations to awaken latent abilities and tap into universal wisdom. I have heard countless stories from fellow travelers who also describe meeting beings of light, star elders, and even playful extraterrestrial entities. Each testimony resonates with the idea that these meetings facilitate a deeper connection to our purpose and the shift toward a higher vibration. It's a reminder that we are not alone in this cosmic journey, and we can reach out and connect with those who are perhaps waiting for us to recognize their existence.

For those seeking to induce their own transformative experiences, cultivating a meditative practice conducive to astral travel can be instrumental. Setting intentions before each session to connect with benevolent beings from the galactic confederation can open doors to extraordinary dimensions. Trusting your intuition and maintaining an open heart may lead to profound encounters that inspire growth and understanding.

Chapter 12: Integration and Reflection

12.1 Processing Your Experiences

Processing encounters with galactic beings requires a blend of mindfulness, creativity, and emotional intelligence. One powerful tool is journaling. Writing down your experiences allows you to capture every detail, feeling, and insight, creating a personal archive that can be revisited. I often spend time with my journal just after an encounter, pouring out my thoughts and emotions on paper. This not only helps in clarifying my experiences but also ensures that I don't lose the nuances of what occurred. Another effective method for processing these mystical moments is engaging in meditation. By quieting the mind, I can connect deeper with the impressions left by the beings I encountered. During meditation, I visualize the experience, reliving it in a safe space that allows me to integrate the lessons learned. Combining visualizations with affirmations can amplify this process. After each contact, I affirm my openness to receiving wisdom and understanding what it all means.

Each encounter with galactic beings has left a mark on my soul, shaping my understanding of existence and our place in the universe. After one particularly vivid experience where I encountered what I can only describe as a celestial being of light, I found myself grappling with immense feelings of love and unity. In that moment, the boundaries of my own life seemed to dissolve, merging into an expansive connection with everything around me. Reflecting on this experience for weeks afterward, I learned that the universe is brimming with opportunities for connection, urging me to shed my fears and embrace the unknown.

The lessons are often simple yet profound. I learned to trust my intuition, recognizing that sometimes our inner voice has a deeper understanding of these cosmic encounters than our rational minds. I have since made a habit of sharing these stories within community circles, connecting with others who resonate with such experiences. Hearing their narratives further solidifies the truth that we are all interconnected, each story weaving together a larger tapestry of understanding about our cosmic neighbors. A practical tip for anyone wanting to deepen their connection is to create a ritual that resonates with you—lighting a candle, using crystals, or even simply sitting in stillness can help ground your energies as you reach out to the galactic realm.

12.2 Lessons Learned from Encounters

Throughout my journeys involving encounters with extraterrestrial presences, I have gathered profound lessons that continue to shape my life in ways I never imagined. The first lesson that stands out is understanding the importance of connection. In every encounter, the overwhelming sense of unity and interconnectedness with the cosmos became apparent. I learned that we are all part of a vast tapestry, woven together by shared energies and intentions. These beings have shown me that even in our deepest struggles, we are never truly alone. This realization has transformed my perspective on relationships, encouraging me to treat all beings with kindness and understanding, regardless of our differences.

These encounters have broadened my understanding of existence beyond the constraints of time and space. I've found that the lessons imparted by these extraterrestrial presences often challenge conventional ideas about reality. They remind me that our human experience is just one layer of a much larger cosmic narrative. This broadened perception encourages a mindset of openness and curiosity, inviting me to explore the infinite possibilities that lie beyond what we can perceive. Embracing this perspective allows me to approach life with wonder and gratitude, fostering a deeper appreciation for every moment and interaction.

As I reflect on these lessons, I offer a practical tip for those looking to connect with these higher realms. Begin by nurturing your inner stillness. Meditation serves as a powerful tool for quieting the mind and welcoming these insights. When you create a space of tranquility, you invite clarity and openness, making it easier to perceive the subtle messages that surround us. In that silence, you may find the wisdom already waiting for you, waiting to be discovered.

12.3 Sharing Your Journey with Others

Sharing my journey has become an essential part of my life and spiritual practice. It fosters a sense of community and support that is vital, especially for those of us who seek the extraordinary, like summoning UFOs or connecting with the Galactic Confederation of Light. Opening up about my experiences creates a ripple effect, where others feel encouraged to share their own stories, fears, and aspirations. Together, we build a collective energy that strengthens our beliefs and intentions. This bond nurtures understanding and acceptance, creating a safe space where we can explore the unknown without judgment. As we share our journeys, we come to realize that we are not alone in our adventures and the thresholds we cross, each story a thread in the grand tapestry of our shared cosmic exploration.

My motivations for sharing my experiences stem from a deep desire to connect with others who resonate with the same cosmic messages I do. Initially, I was hesitant, feeling vulnerable about revealing my encounters and insights. However, each time I opened up, I found not only acceptance but powerful validation. There's magic in storytelling, especially when it pertains to something as wondrous as extraterrestrial encounters or spiritual awakenings. My experiences range from moments of breathtaking beauty during meditations under the stars to startling communications that shook my understanding of reality. Each story I told inspired others to step forward and share their own, creating a dialogue filled with enthusiasm and wonder. It became clear to me that sharing my journey wasn't just about me; it was about uplifting a community and affirming our connection to something greater than ourselves.

In sharing these moments, I've discovered that vulnerability often gives way to empowerment. Engaging with others who have similar experiences can lead to transformative insights and collective growth. By honestly recounting my interactions with the ethereal and the mysterious, I hope to encourage others to reflect on their own paths and maybe even take bold steps toward their own experiences with the galactic realms. For those who are just beginning their journey or feel hesitant, remember that every story is valid and holds energy that can spark inspiration in others. Start small—share a thought, a feeling, or a moment that moved you. You may find that your willingness to be open will draw in like-minded souls, creating a web of support and shared discovery. Reach out, connect, and allow the magic of community to enhance your journey.

Chapter 13: The Future of Humanity and Galactic Involvement

13.1 The Shift in Human Consciousness

This current shift in global consciousness feels like an awakening, a collective rise in awareness that transcends borders and belief systems. Everywhere I look, there seems to be a deeper yearning for connection—not just with each other but with the universe itself. More people are opening their minds and hearts to the idea that we are not alone, and this burgeoning awareness is noticeable. Conversations about UFOs and extraterrestrial intelligence are becoming more commonplace, moving from the fringe to the forefront of mainstream discussion. It's as if a veil is lifting, allowing for the recognition that we are part of a much larger cosmic community. As we grapple with the implications of our existence, the fabric of society is starting to weave in these extraordinary threads of thought, leading to transformative revelations about our identity, purpose, and role in the cosmos.

In my own experience, contact with beings from beyond has been a pivotal aspect of my personal journey. These contact experiences, whether direct or indirect, are a catalyst for understanding the fundamental interconnectedness of all life. Each encounter, every communication, brings forward waves of knowledge that resonate at a vibrational level, prompting me to shift my perspective and embrace a broader reality. The feelings of love and acceptance I've felt during these experiences reinforce my belief that we are all being invited to participate in this shift. It's a collective call to awaken. As I share my encounters, I see the same spark ignite in others—their curiosity peaks, and they begin to explore their own capabilities of connecting with the Galactic Confederation of Light. This is more than just theoretical discussion; it's a living, breathing experience that brings me closer to both the cosmos and my fellow humans.

To engage with this shift, I recommend creating a space for open dialogue about these experiences with friends and family, fostering an environment of curiosity rather than skepticism. Practice meditative techniques that enhance your intuitive abilities, allowing for clearer reception of messages from the universe. By grounding yourself and maintaining a positive vibration, you will find it easier to connect with higher realms of consciousness and, potentially, those celestial beings who wish to communicate. We are all participants in this extraordinary journey toward expanded awareness, and each step we take in understanding our place in the universe brings us closer to the truth of our existence.

13.2 Ways the Galactic Federation Assists Us

The Galactic Federation plays a critical role in supporting humanity as we navigate this complex journey of evolution and awakening. One of the most significant support systems they provide is through direct communication and guidance. Many people, including myself, have experienced encounters that seem tailor-made to enlighten our understanding of interstellar existence. These beings share knowledge not just about the cosmos but about our own capabilities. They encourage us to tap into our inner potential and elevate our consciousness, often through meditation and energetic practices that resonate with the universal laws of love and peace.

Additionally, the Galactic Federation facilitates healing on multiple levels. They assist us in releasing old traumas and harmful patterns that have kept humanity in cycles of suffering. I've personally felt the shift in my energy during meditations where their presence is felt. This is more than mere spiritual support; it's a tangible experience. I often perceive waves of warm energy that cleanse my aura, helping me to reclaim a state of balance and harmony. Their technologies, often beyond our current understanding, are shared where appropriate, allowing us access to advanced healing methods not available on Earth.

Mutual growth between humans and galactic beings has become a beautiful dance of sharing and learning. As I have interacted with these celestial entities, I've noticed how they reflect the best parts of ourselves back to us. Their journey has been one of overcoming challenges that mirror our own, allowing us to learn from their experiences. The Galactic Federation invites us to see ourselves as part of a larger family, bending the boundaries of time and space. This connection helps cultivate a vision where collaboration, rather than competition, leads the way. To tap into this reality, try engaging in regular meditative practices that focus on creating an open channel for communication with these benevolent beings. Contemplating the idea of unity with the cosmos can shift your focus and create a path for deeper understanding and cooperation.

13.3 Preparing for a New Era of Intergalactic Relations

Humanity stands on the precipice of a new chapter in our cosmic saga, where expanded interactions with galactic civilizations could become a reality. To truly prepare for these encounters, we must embrace an open-minded approach that prioritizes understanding and connection. This begins with fostering a collective curiosity about the universe and our place within it. We need to cultivate a sense of wonder about what lies beyond our own world, encouraging not just scientific exploration but also spiritual and philosophical discussions about existence, consciousness, and our shared journey among the stars. Engaging in community conversations can help demystify the unknown, inviting diverse perspectives on potential interactions with extraterrestrial beings.

One of the most significant aspects of preparing for these interactions is developing a mindset of love and compassion. I envision a world where humanity projects positivity and goodwill toward higher beings. This involves not only being receptive to their presence but also actively working on ourselves to cultivate harmony within. It can mean practicing meditation and mindfulness to raise our vibrational frequencies, making us more attuned to the subtle energies of the universe. By fostering an environment of peace and respect, we create an energetic space of connection, inviting not just communication but meaningful friendships with galactic friends. Each of us has the power to visualize and manifest this new era, not only through our thoughts but also through our actions, intentions, and how we treat each other as we step into this vast unknown.

As we embrace this journey to meeting and uniting with galactic beings, practical steps can aid our intentions. One simple yet powerful method is establishing a dedicated space for meditation or connection, free of distractions, where we can invite our cosmic counterparts to join us. Lighting a candle, playing soft music, or even using crystals can enhance the energy in the room. As we meditate, visualizing bright, loving beams of light surrounding us can help broaden our connection to higher realms and encourage open communication with these civilizations. This conscious act of inviting spiritual energy into our lives sets the stage for a welcoming environment, ready for the wonders that await us beyond the stars.

Chapter 14: Debunking Myths Around UFOs and Summoning

14.1 Common Misconceptions About UFOs

Many people harbor misconceptions about UFOs, often shaped by sensationalized media portrayals and a lack of firsthand experiences. One prevalent myth is that all UFO sightings must involve extraterrestrial spacecraft. While the term UFO simply refers to any unidentified flying object, it does not automatically imply an alien origin. Many reported sightings can be attributed to natural phenomena, human-made objects, or atmospheric anomalies. These misunderstandings tend to cloud genuine inquiry into the UFO phenomenon. In my own journey, I've encountered various forms of aerial anomalies, some of which defied easy explanation. However, my experiences highlight the importance of separating what is truly unknown from what is simply misunderstood. UFOs can represent many things, and it's essential to approach the subject with an open mind rather than jumping to conclusions based on preconceived notions.

Reflecting on my personal encounters, I realized that misinformation can easily spread, often overshadowing the genuine experiences people have. For instance, during one particularly memorable night, I witnessed an extraordinary light in the sky that moved in ways I couldn't explain. It was easy to dismiss it or label it as an alien craft, but my understanding deepened when I researched more about aerial phenomena. Engaging with research allowed me to approach my experiences from an informed perspective, which revealed how often our perceptions can deceive us. I urge others to share their experiences openly, as this can cultivate a community of seekers who learn from one another. As we explore and discuss our encounters, we contribute to a broader understanding that transcends myths and focuses on genuine exploration.

Staying curious and informed is vital as you delve into the world of UFOs. When trying to summon UFOs or connect with the Galactic Confederation of Light, consider keeping a journal of your observations and feelings. This can clarify your thoughts and aid in recognizing patterns over time. Remember that many experiences may not fit neatly into societal expectations, and that's perfectly acceptable. Your openness and willingness to explore the unknown might just attract the very encounters you seek.

14.2 Discerning Truth from Disinformation

In a world so saturated with information, finding the truth can feel like searching for a needle in a haystack, especially when many voices shout louder than the whisper of authenticity. One of the techniques I've found useful in separating fact from the noise of disinformation lies in the art of critical thinking. It's essential to question the sources of information I encounter. I often ask myself who is presenting this information and what their motivations might be. If a story seems too outrageous to be true, or if it caters to fears and biases, I take a moment to pause and scrutinize it. I look for corroboration across multiple reputable sources and try to discern patterns that align with established knowledge or shared experiences within my community. True insights, especially about phenomena like UFOs and the galactic confederation, tend to resonate deeply and harmoniously with other aspects of spiritual awareness and personal experiences.

Throughout my own journey, I faced numerous challenges that tested my ability to differentiate what felt real from what seemed fabricated. There was a time when I was heavily influenced by sensational videos and articles that promised the secrets of UFO sightings and connections with otherworldly beings. I became frustrated when my own experiences didn't mirror those grand narratives. Feeling lost in a sea of conflicting accounts, I realized I needed to ground myself in my experiences rather than rely solely on others' perspectives. Documenting my own observations and feelings in a journal became a lifeline. It helped me connect dots that senseless articles revolved around, revealing patterns and truths that were very personal. My process evolved into a more balanced blend of intuition and reason, fostering an understanding that truth is often layered and complex.

As I navigated through the disinformation landscape, I developed practices that helped keep my focus on what was real and resonant for me. One effective tip is to engage in community discussions with those who share similar interests. Sharing experiences often reveals hidden truths that individual searches might overlook. By surrounding myself with mindful individuals, I learn from their encounters, leading to an enriched understanding of both the cosmic and personal. In cultivating an open mind while remaining skeptical of sensational narratives, I allow room for genuine discovery and growth. Remember, it's not merely about filtering out deceit but about encouraging the exploration of our consciousness together in the search for authenticity.

14.3 The Importance of Critical Thinking

Embracing a critical mindset is essential when delving into the mysteries of UFOs and galactic phenomena. In a field rife with speculation, sensational stories, and sometimes deliberate confusion, applying critical thinking helps to differentiate between genuine experiences and mere flights of fancy. By scrutinizing information and questioning the sources, we sharpen our ability to discern the truth. I have learned that exploring the unknown requires not just an open mind, but a questioning spirit. When I first began looking into UFO sightings and their connections to the galactic confederation of light, I faced countless claims that seemed unbelievable. However, by meticulously evaluating each account and considering its context, I was able to navigate the sea of information more effectively. This approach allowed me to engage with the subject seriously while remaining grounded.

In my journey, I have encountered moments where critical thinking illuminated the path ahead. For instance, during one of my first group meditations aimed at summoning interstellar beings, I noticed the variance in our intentions and expectations. While some participants were full of hope and excitement for a tangible experience, others approached the session with skepticism. I found myself in the middle, feeling the energy of the room shift. Using critical thought, I began connecting the dots—our intentions were influencing the experience, and it wasn't just about who was most fervently hopeful. Reflecting on this, I encouraged my group to align our thoughts and intentions, which ultimately led to a more fruitful and enriching experience. This taught me that critical thinking doesn't just involve analysis; it also encompasses emotional and energetic awareness.

Developing a habit of critical thinking can transform your exploration of UFOs and galactic energies. Always take the time to question your beliefs and the narratives surrounding them. Embrace curiosity but balance it with discernment. As you look into your own experiences or stories shared by others, remember to assess their validity through the lens of critical inquiry. Keep a journal documenting your thoughts and emotions during your explorations. This practice can help clarify your intentions and reveal patterns that may not be immediately apparent. In a world filled with mystery and wonder, critical thinking is your compass, guiding you toward deeper understanding and connection.

Chapter 15: Continuing the Journey Beyond Contact

15.1 Staying Open to Future Experiences

Staying open to future experiences is more than just a mindset; it's a brave practice that invites exploration into the vast unknown. When I first began my journey into the world of UFOs and the Galactic Confederation of Light, I quickly realized that the willingness to embrace the uncertainties and possibilities that lay ahead was essential. Each encounter holds the potential to reveal something significant, and if I were to close myself off, I would miss out on extraordinary moments that could expand my understanding of the universe. Keeping an open heart and mind allows me to connect with energies beyond our earthly realm and fosters a welcoming atmosphere for contact.

I've learned that curiosity is a powerful catalyst for growth. Every time I meditate or take part in a gathering focused on summoning extraterrestrial energies, I dare to confront my own fears. What if I experienced something I couldn't explain? What if I came face-to-face with a being from another dimension? Each thought pushes me to embrace the idea that beyond fear lies wonder and potential. This bravery to face the unknown has become one of my most cherished practices, as it not only enhances my connection with the cosmos but also deepens my understanding of who I am and what I seek in life.

As my journey unfolds, each new experience prepares me for even greater adventures. I find that my openness to the unknown cultivates a sense of trust in the universe. With every channeling session or lightworker gathering, I sprinkle seeds of awareness into my subconscious, allowing me to adapt to ever-changing encounters. This process is akin to creating a fabric woven with diverse threads of experiences, each one contributing to my evolving tapestry of understanding. The more I explore, the more I realize that each UFO sighting, each message from the Galactic Confederation provides invaluable lessons that shape my perspective and readiness for future events.

Embracing the unknown requires a willingness to learn and grow. I've learned to trust my instincts and intuition, keeping them finely tuned as I venture into unexplored territory. Each challenge I face strengthens my resolve, reminding me that every experience, positive or negative, contributes to my journey. Inspired by this knowledge, I continuously ask for guidance, aligning my intentions with the energies around me. The key takeaway is to remain actively curious and to embrace each opportunity for growth. Whether it's a meditation session or an unexpected encounter under the stars, the universe has a way of leading us toward revelations that transform our understanding of existence.

15.2 Building a Community of Like-Minded Souls

The power of creating supportive networks cannot be overstated, especially for those of us who are passionate about summoning UFOs and connecting with the Galactic Confederation of Light. These networks provide a safe haven where we can exchange ideas, share experiences, and nurture our growth. Together, we form a web of understanding that transcends the limitations of individual inquiry. In these spaces, we can explore the vast universe within and around us, bolstering our confidence and amplifying our efforts to reach out to higher realms. It's in the company of fellow enthusiasts that I've found a sense of belonging, making the quest for knowledge and connection feel less daunting and infinitely more exciting.

One of the most valuable lessons I've learned through building this community is the art of patience and persistence. Engaging with like-minded souls reminds me that every effort we make is a stepping stone toward something greater. Whether it's through meditation, intention setting, or using specific frequencies to tune into the cosmic vibrations, it's the mutual support that often leads to breakthroughs. So, as you consider your own path within this realm, look for those connections that resonate with you. Seek out others who share your goals and dreams. Together, you can amplify your journey and pave the way for extraordinary experiences. Remember, the universe thrives on cooperation, and through our collective energy, we can reach new heights.

15.3 Expanding Your Cosmic Awareness

Expanding consciousness and understanding our cosmic place requires ongoing dedication to practices that elevate our awareness. One of the most effective ways I have discovered is through meditation. By stilling the mind and tuning into the vibrations around us, we can open our hearts and minds to the truth of the universe. I often visualize myself in a vast cosmic space, surrounded by the stars, feeling the energy of the galactic confederation enveloping me. This not only calms my spirit but also heightens my sensitivity to the energies of extraterrestrial beings. Journaling can also aid in this quest. Writing about my experiences and feelings helps clarify thoughts that connect me with the universe's mysteries. Over time, I've learned to recognize signs and synchronicities that suggest I'm on the right path, further deepening my cosmic connection.

In my journey, I've embraced the practice of star gazing, allowing myself to get lost in the beauty and vastness of the night sky. When I look up at the stars, I send out vibrations of love and gratitude, inviting communication with beings from other realms. This act of intentional connection has opened doors to profound experiences where I've felt the presence of UFOs in the distance, guiding me toward greater truths. I also participate in group meditations focused on inviting the energies of the galactic confederation. The synergy created by collective intentions amplifies our ability to reach higher frequencies, enhancing our shared journey into consciousness. Understanding how to align with the universe through breathing techniques and visualizations enables me to feel more in tune with the energies that surround us.

As you embark on your path of cosmic expansion, remember that the universe is listening. Take a moment each day to express your intentions and desires. Whether it's through silent prayers, affirmations, or even spontaneous moments of gratitude, every act of acknowledgment magnifies your connection to the cosmos. Consider creating a sacred space in your home, adorned with items that resonate with the energies you wish to attract, fostering an environment conducive to the expansion of your awareness. This practice has transformed my home into a peaceful sanctuary, making it easier to connect with the higher realms. Ultimately, trust that the universe is unfolding as it should, and your efforts will be met with signs and messages guiding your journey.

Also by Jessie Contreras

Messages from the Stars: A Guide to Summoning the Galactic
Federation
Celestial Awakening: Ascension and the Art of Summoning UFOs
Energy Vortexes: Harnessing Power for UFO Summoning
The Alien Code: Unlocking the Matrix
The Ultimate UFO Summoning Guide:2026 Edition
How To Master The Ancient Art Of Summoning Motherships
The Resonant Universe: Bioelectrical Energy And The Call Of UFOs
UFOs and the Art of Mimicry: The Hidden Intelligence Behind the
Disguise

About the Author

Jessie Contreras is a dedicated researcher of unidentified aerial phenomena whose work blends disciplined observation with an interest in how human consciousness shapes extraordinary experiences. Guided by a lifelong fascination with the night sky, he shares his insights through community work, educational content, and continued study. His mission is to explore the phenomenon with clarity, integrity, and an unwavering commitment to understanding what lies beyond the familiar.

About the Publisher

Summon UFOs is a forward-thinking publishing brand dedicated to exploring the intersection of consciousness, extraterrestrial contact, and human potential. Through its works, the brand presents innovative perspectives on UFO phenomena, blending experiential practices, emerging technologies, and esoteric knowledge into a cohesive framework for understanding and initiating contact. Summon UFOs aims to inspire curiosity, expand awareness, and empower individuals to engage with the unknown in a structured, intentional, and transformative way.